Water Everywhere

FIRST EDITION
Series Editor Deborah Lock; **US Editor** John Searcy; **Managing Art Editor** Rachael Foster;
Art Editor Gemma Fletcher; **DTP Designer** Emma Hansen-Knarhoi; **Pre-Production Producer** Nadine King;
Producer Sara Hu; **Picture Researcher** Rob Nunn; **Jacket Designer** Simon Oon;
Reading Consultant Linda Gambrell, PhD

THIS EDITION
Editorial Management by Oriel Square
Produced for DK by WonderLab Group LLC
Jennifer Emmett, Erica Green, Kate Hale, *Founders*

Editors Grace Hill Smith, Libby Romero, Michaela Weglinski;
Photography Editors Kelley Miller, Annette Kiesow, Nicole DiMella; **Managing Editor** Rachel Houghton;
Designers Project Design Company; **Researcher** Michelle Harris; **Copy Editor** Lori Merritt;
Indexer Connie Binder; **Proofreader** Larry Shea; **Reading Specialist** Dr. Jennifer Albro;
Curriculum Specialist Elaine Larson

Published in the United States by DK Publishing
1745 Broadway, 20th Floor, New York, NY 10019

22 23 24 25 26 10 9 8 7 6 5 4 3 2 1
001-333459-May/2023

Published in Great Britain by Dorling Kindersley Limited

A catalog record for this book
is available from the Library of Congress.
HC ISBN: 978-0-7440-6809-2
PB ISBN: 978-0-7440-6810-8

Printed and bound in China

The publisher would like to thank the following for their kind permission to reproduce their images:
a=above; c=center; b=below; l=left; r=right; t=top; b/g=background

Shutterstock.com: Lotta Axing 15tl, Nokwan007 19c, Stephan Pawloski 24, slowmotiongli 17t; zombiu26 11

Cover images: *Front:* **Dreamstime.com:** Easyshutter b, Geraktv (Rain), Sureshr; *Back:* **Dreamstime.com:** Milo827 bl, Larry Rains cra; *Spine:* **Dreamstime.com:** Easyshutter

All other images © Dorling Kindersley

For more information see: www.dkimages.com

For the curious
www.dk.com

Level 2

Water Everywhere

Jill Atkins

Contents

Water!

We use lots of water every day. We take baths and brush our teeth. We water the yard. We wash our dishes, our clothes, and our cars.

We go swimming and play water sports.

Washing Hands
We wash our hands before meals so we don't get germs on our food that can make us sick.

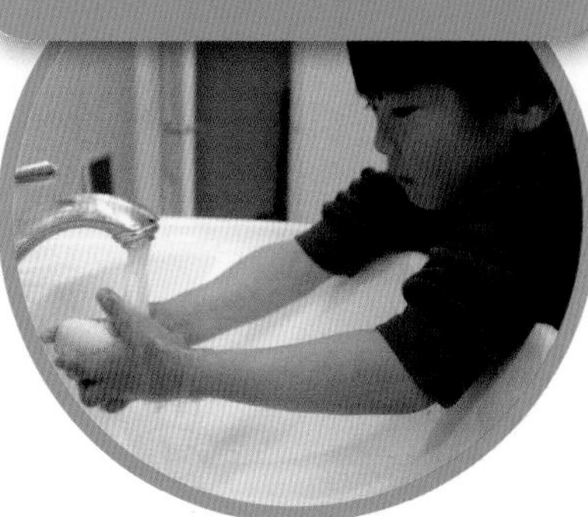

We also need water. We have to drink water every day to keep our bodies healthy and alert.

Water
is the best
thing to drink
between
meals.

Earth's Water

Almost three-quarters of planet Earth is covered in water.
Most of the water is contained in five large oceans and several small seas.

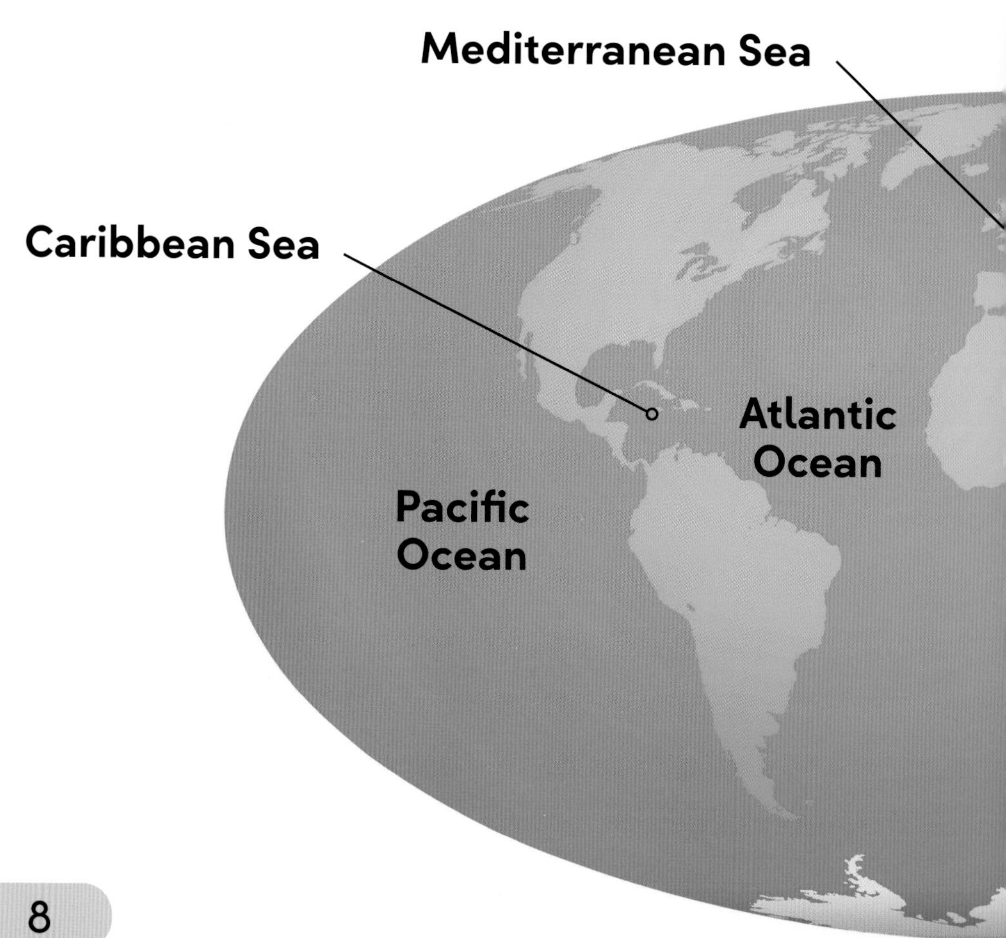

We cannot drink this water, because it is too salty. It would make us sick to drink it.
So, how does this water become the water we use and need?

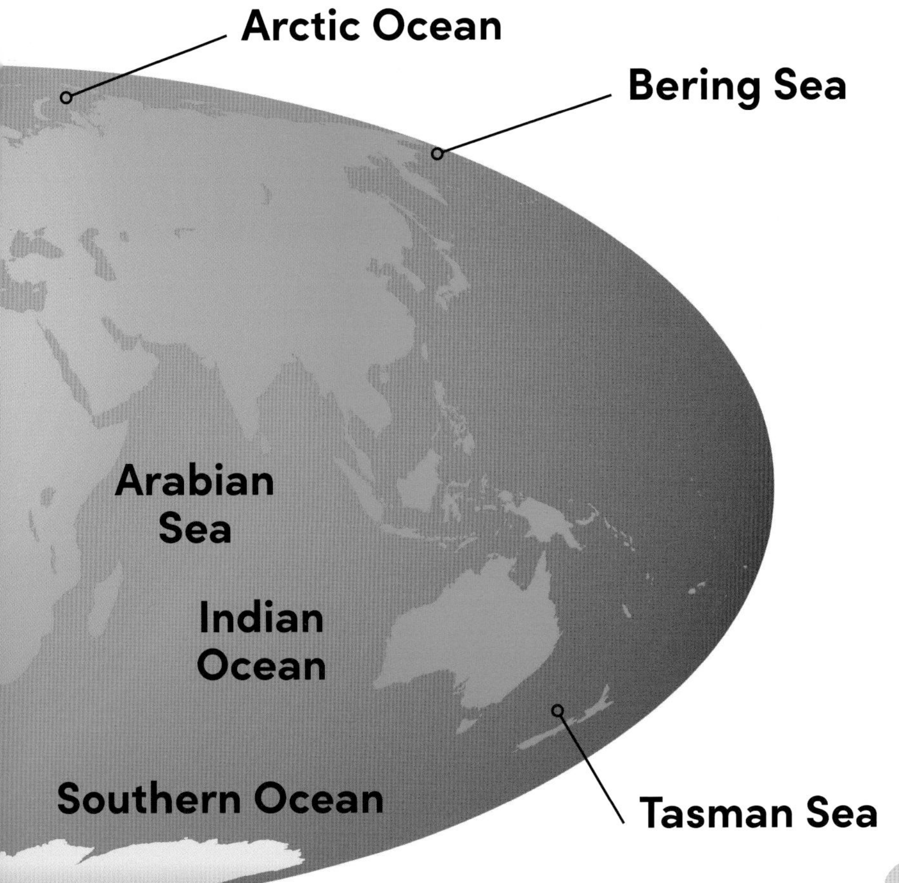

The Water Cycle

Water in the oceans and seas is warmed by the sun.
The heated water becomes droplets that rise up and form clouds.
The wind blows the clouds over the land.
Then, the water cools and falls from the clouds as rain.

Snowflakes
In cold weather, water from clouds falls as sleet, hail, or snow. Each snowflake has a different pattern with six points.

Rainwater is called freshwater because it is no longer salty. Some rainwater runs into rivers, which flow into lakes or back into the sea.

This process is called the water cycle.

Water for People

The water we use comes from lakes, rivers, or natural springs under the ground.
It is cleaned so it is fit to drink.
Underground pipes carry the water into our homes.

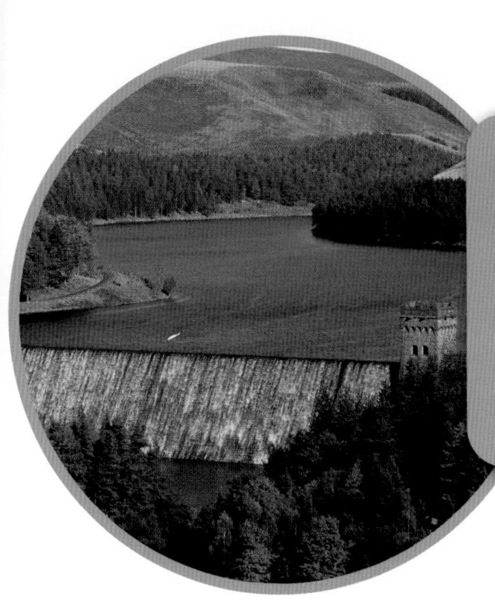

Storing Water
Sometimes, a dam is built across a river to make a reservoir. Some of the water we use is stored there.

It is important that we do not waste water. Adults can help save water by fixing leaky pipes. You can help by remembering to turn off faucets.

Water for Animals

Animals also need water
for drinking and bathing.
Elephants can suck more than
2 gallons (7.5 liters) of water
into their long trunks.
They squirt this water
into their mouths to drink or
over their backs to keep cool.

The Arabian, or dromedary, camel is nicknamed "ship of the desert."

Camels can store water in their bodies. They can live more than five days in the desert without a drink.

Many creatures live in the ocean and cannot survive without water around them. Some hunt or hide in deep water where it is cool and dark. Others swim near the surface, searching for other animals to eat.

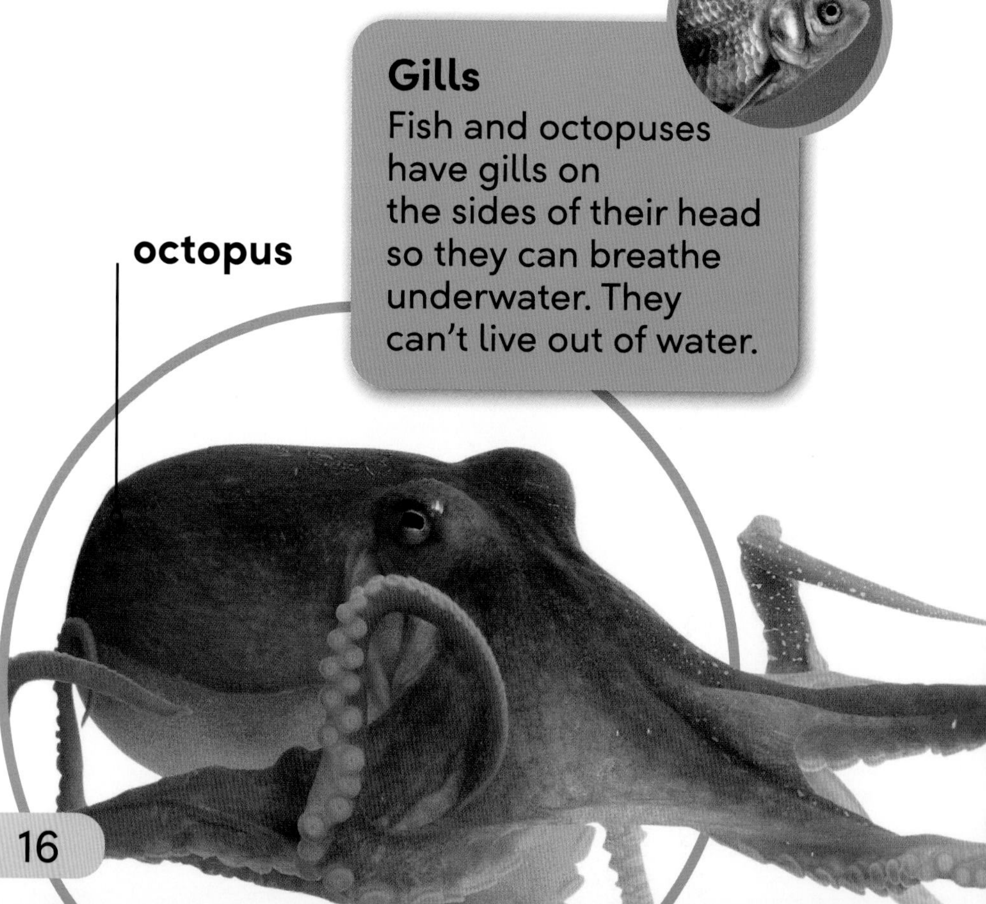

Gills

Fish and octopuses have gills on the sides of their head so they can breathe underwater. They can't live out of water.

Some whales, such as the humpback whale, eat millions of tiny creatures called plankton.
These whales have long comb-like bristles instead of teeth.

Water for Plants

Plants need water to grow. Their roots push down under the soil to find water. They take in water through their roots.

A cactus can grow in the dry desert because it stores water for a long time.

Rice only grows in fields that are covered in water. If there isn't enough rain, farmers add water to keep the fields wet.

Forces of Nature

In some places,
there is so much rain
that it causes floods.
People's homes can be
washed away.

In other places,
there is sometimes
hardly any rain at all.
This is called a drought.

On December 26, 2004, an earthquake in the Indian Ocean triggered the deadliest tsunami in recorded history.

Sometimes, water becomes a dangerous power.
For example, strong currents in the sea can wash people away.
The most powerful form of water is a tsunami [sue-NAH-mee], a giant wave.

Forms of Water

Water looks different when it gets very cold or hot. The water we drink is liquid. As water becomes very cold, it freezes.

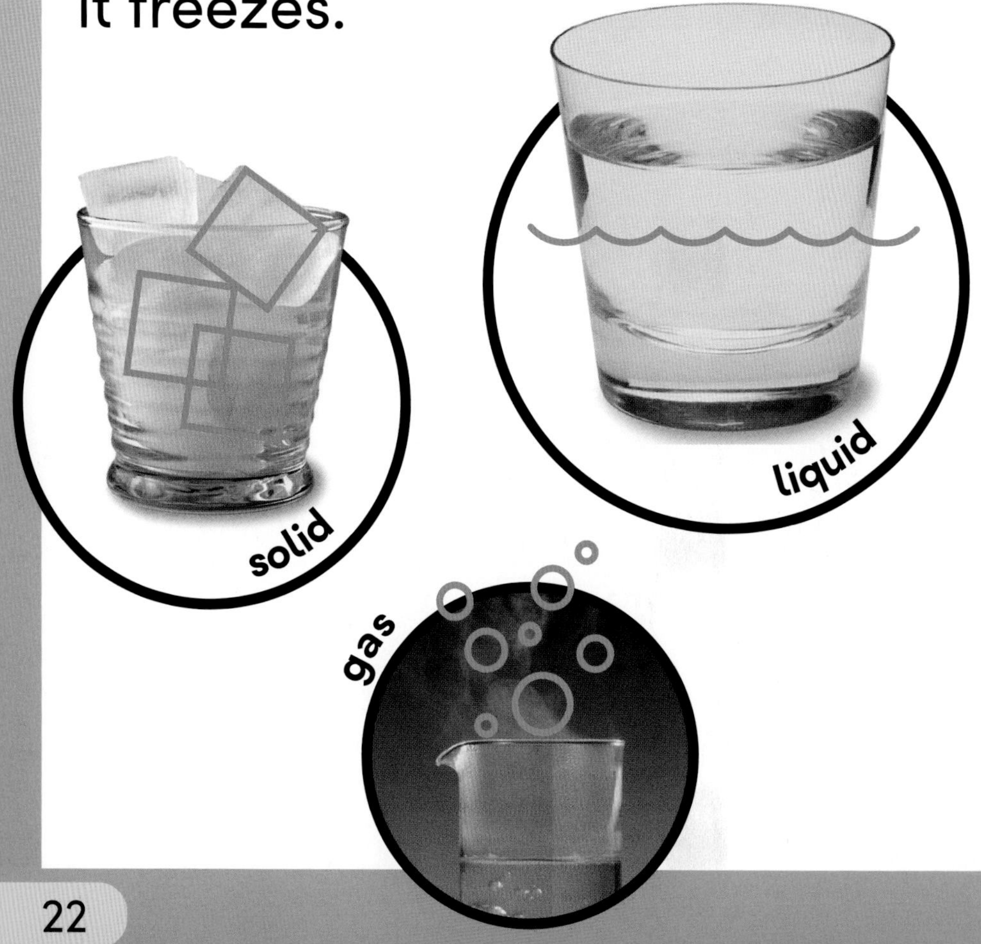

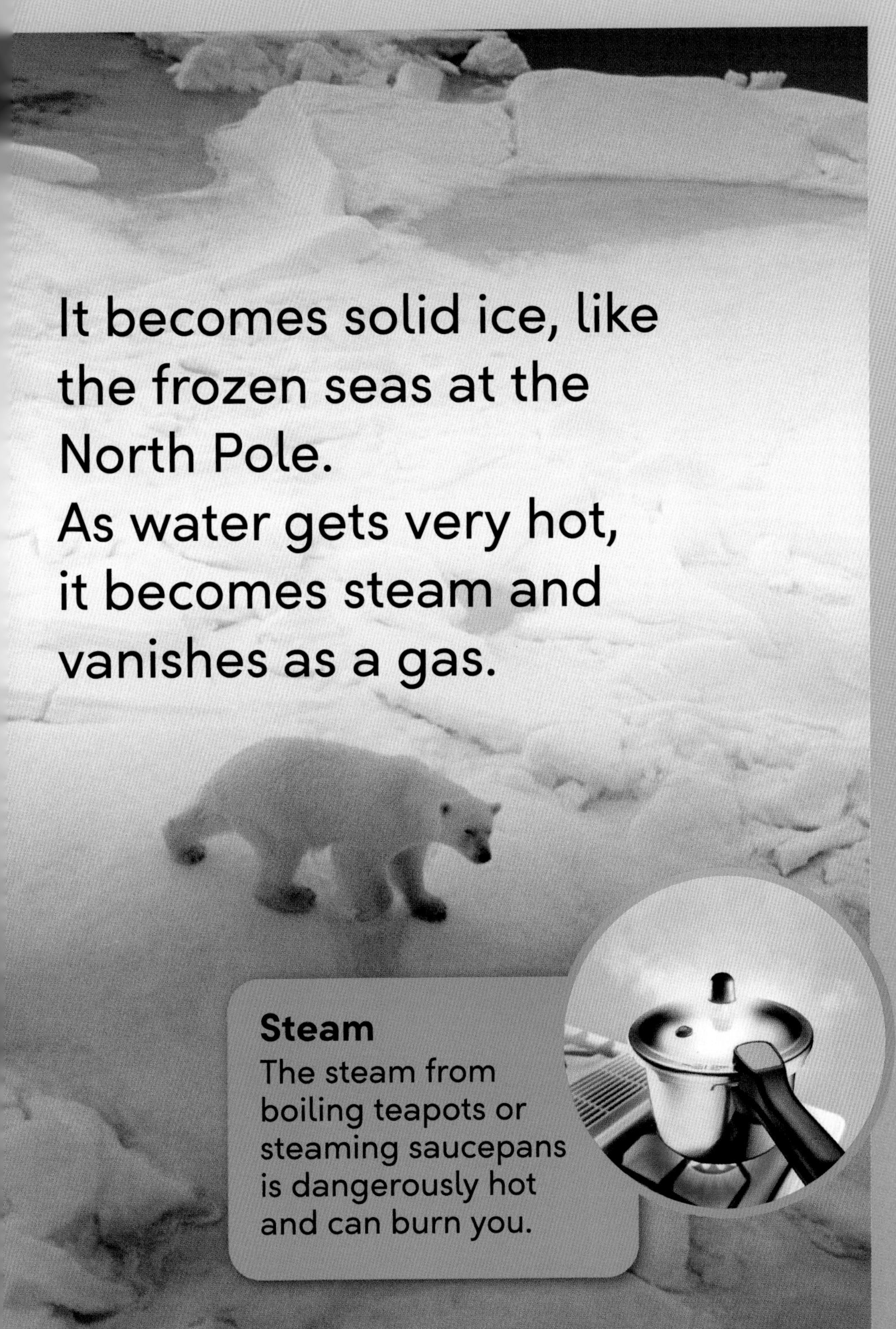

It becomes solid ice, like the frozen seas at the North Pole.
As water gets very hot, it becomes steam and vanishes as a gas.

Steam
The steam from boiling teapots or steaming saucepans is dangerously hot and can burn you.

Water as Power

Water can be used to move and power machines. The wheels and cogs of a water mill are turned by water.

The Brilliant Dam and Generating Station are in British Columbia, Canada. They use water to make electricity.

The Rocket
One of the earliest steam-powered trains was the Rocket. George Stephenson invented it in 1829.

Rushing water is sometimes used to make electricity.

Steam has been used to power machines for more than 250 years. In a steam engine, water is heated in a large tank to make steam. The steam is used to make the engine go.

Keeping It Clean

It's important to keep the world's water clean. If a ship carrying oil crashes into rocks, oil pours out into the sea and harms the wildlife.

bird coated in oil

At least 1,500 birds died after the Braer oil tanker ran aground off the Shetland Islands, Scotland, in 1993.

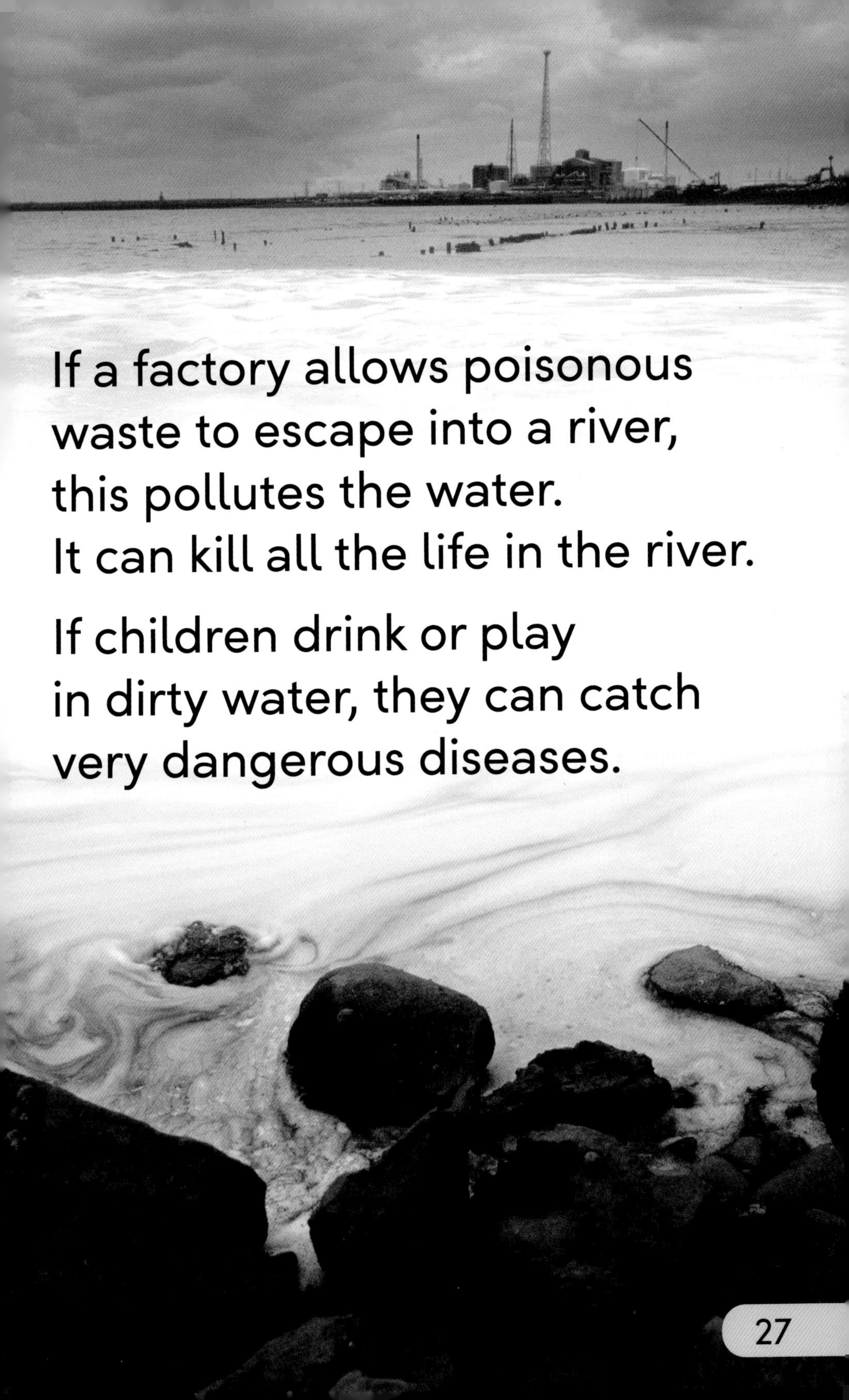

If a factory allows poisonous
waste to escape into a river,
this pollutes the water.
It can kill all the life in the river.

If children drink or play
in dirty water, they can catch
very dangerous diseases.

On Earth and in Space

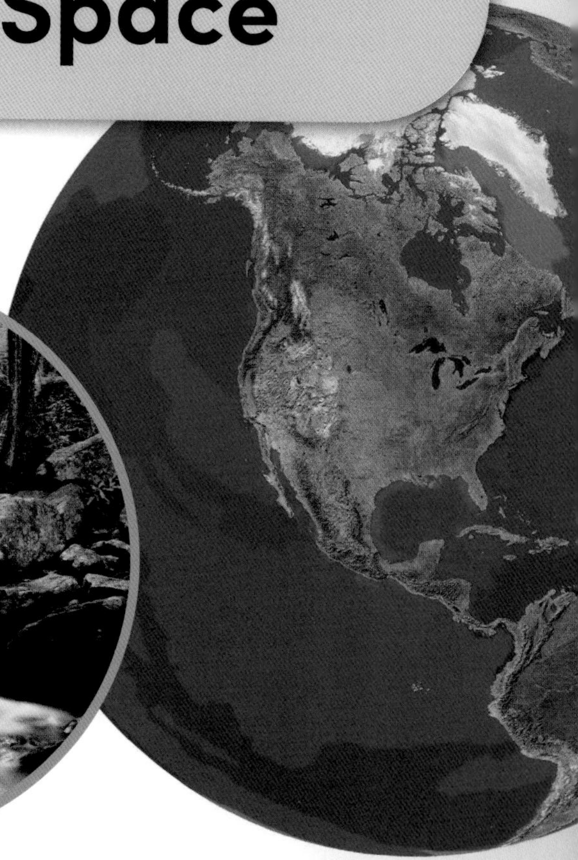

Water is very important to every living thing. Without it, no humans, animals, or plants could exist on this planet.

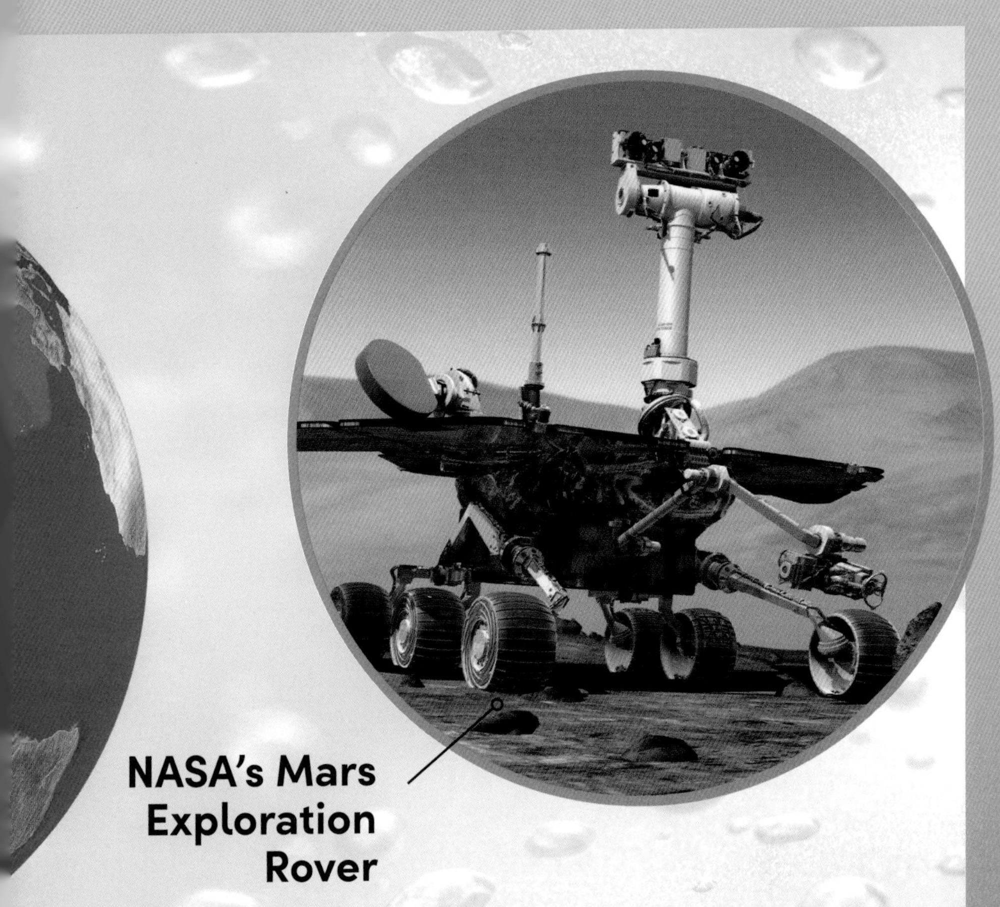

NASA's Mars Exploration Rover

Scientists and astronauts have been exploring other planets like Mars for signs of water. If they find water, it might mean that life exists or used to exist out there in space!

Glossary

Dam
A large wall that stops the flow of a river

Drought
When an area gets less than its normal amount of rain for a long period of time

Flood
A huge flow of water on normally dry land

Freshwater
Water that is not salty

Pollute
When waste and chemicals harm Earth's air, water, and land

Reservoir
A body of water that is being stored for various uses

Tsunami
A giant wave

Water cycle
The process of water moving between the air and land

Index

Quiz

Answer the questions to see what you have learned. Check your answers in the key below.

1. How much of Earth is covered in water?
2. Why can't we drink ocean water?
3. Which part of a plant takes in water?
4. What are the three forms of water?
5. True or False: Scientists have explored other planets for signs of water.

1. Three-quarters 2. It's too salty 3. The roots
4. Solid, liquid, and gas 5. True